CHANGING WORLD
IRAN

CHANGING WORLD

IRAN

Richard Dargie

ARCTURUS

This edition first published by Arcturus Publishing
Distributed by Black Rabbit Books
P.O. Box 3263
Mankato
Minnesota MN 56002

Printed in the United States

Library of Congress Cataloging-in-Publication Data

Dargie, Richard.
  Iran / Richard Dargie.
     p. cm. -- (Changing world)
  ISBN 978-1-84837-007-4
  1. Iran--Juvenile literature. I. Title.

  DS254.75.D37 2009
  955--dc22

                       2008016657

Series concept: Alex Woolf
Editor and picture researcher: Cath Senker
Designer: Ian Winton
Illustrator: Stefan Chabluk

Picture credits:
Corbis: cover left (Kazyoshi Nomachi), cover right (Kazyoshi Nomachi), 6 (George Steinmetz), 7, 8 (Roger Wood), 11
(Kazyoshi Nomachi), 13, 14 (Arthur Thévenart), 18 (Touhig Sion/Corbis Sygma), 20 (David Turnley), 23 (Abedin
Taherkenareh/epa), 37 (George Steinmetz), 39 (Lynsey Addario), 40 (Ceerwan Aziz/Reuters), 41 (Mikhail Klimentiev/epa),
43 (Reuters).
Getty Images: 16 (Time & Life Pictures), 17 (AFP), 25 (AFP), 26, 29 (AFP), 30 (AFP), 33 (AFP), 34 (Scott Peterson).
Shutterstock: 36 (Shelley Shay).

The illustrations on pages 9, 10, 19, 22, 27, 31, and 32 are by Stefan Chabluk.

Cover captions:
Left: Worshippers pray at the shrine of Imam Reza, the eighth Shia imam, in Mashhad, Iran.
Right: The Azadi Tower, built in 1971, marks the entrance to the city of Tehran.

Contents

CHAPTER 1

The Land of Iran

Iran is a land of snow-capped mountains, high pasture, and desert plains. For thousands of years, Iran has been home to one of the oldest civilizations in the world. Modern Iranians are proud of their country's long history and its culture. Today, Iran is a strong regional power that controls one of the most important locations on the globe.

Where is Iran?

Iran lies in the southwestern corner of Asia and is flanked by seven neighbors. To the north, Iran is bordered by Armenia, Azerbaijan, and Turkmenistan. On its western side, Iran shares a frontier with Iraq in the south and with Turkey in the north. Iran's eastern neighbors are Pakistan and Afghanistan.

COMPARING COUNTRIES: HOW BIG IS IRAN?

Land area:

Iran	642,796 sq mi (1,648,195 sq km)
United States	3,832,386 sq mi (9,826,630 sq km)
France	214,890 sq mi (551,000sq km)
Germany	139,230 sq mi (357,000 sq km)
United Kingdom	94,380 sq mi (242,900sq km)

Source: *CIA World Factbook*, 2008

Water forms an important part of Iran's border. Almost 403 mi (650 km) of Iran's northern frontier runs along the shore of the Caspian Sea,

The unusual hills and dunes along Iran's southeastern coast have been shaped by the baking sun and the monsoon rains. The area here is sparsely populated. Most people in this part of Iran live in a few small fishing villages and ports.

while almost all of Iran's long southern border is made up of the waters of the Persian Gulf and the Gulf of Oman. Thanks to its size and location, Iran is one of the most important countries in the area known as the Middle East.

Landscape

Iran is a very mountainous country. The Zagros Mountains cut across western Iran from north to south, reaching heights of over 13,120 ft (4,000 m). The pyramid peak of Mount Damavand rises in the northern chain of the Alborz Mountains above the Caspian coast. At 18,400 ft (5,610 m), this sleeping volcano is one of the highest mountains in Asia.

Broad basins or plateaus lie between the mountain peaks. Much of central Iran is covered by a high plateau that sits at over 2,950 ft (900 m) above sea level. Many of Iran's towns and

Although covered in snow for much of the year, the summit of Mount Damavand in northern Iran emits steam and volcanic gases such as sulfur dioxide. The ancient Persians believed that a fire-breathing dragon lived within the volcanic peak.

villages have grown up around the more fertile areas in these basins. To the east of the central plateau, however, lie two vast salt deserts, which are largely uninhabited except for a few scattered oases. Here, the dry, stony land is covered with sand and marked with outcrops of salt where the marshes have dried out in the sun.

There is little low-lying land in Iran. However, the small but heavily irrigated Khuzestan plain on Iran's western border with Iraq is one of the most fertile areas in the Middle East. There are also smaller plains in the narrow gap between the high Alborz peaks and the waters of the Caspian Sea.

Climate

Iran is an arid or dry land with little rain, although it is more humid along the northern and southern coasts. In the Zagros and Alborz mountains, the winters are bitterly cold, with temperatures often below 32°F (0°C) and frequent snow on the higher slopes. By high summer, the snow has melted, leaving the bare rock peaks exposed.

In central Iran, summer temperatures can rise from the high 90s to 120°F (high 30s and 40s °C) Much of the country receives less than 10 inches (25 cm) of rain each year, falling to less than 4 inches (10 cm) in the deserts. In the hotter parts of Iran, the streams and rivers are often seasonal

CASE STUDY: IRAN'S SHRINKING LAKE

Over 87 mi (140 km) long and 40 mi (55 km) wide, Lake Urmia is Iran's largest lake. Although filled by snowmelt each spring, Urmia has been shrinking for years because of evaporation in the summer heat. Owing to the high salt levels in its water, fish cannot live in the lake, but humans have collected the salt and used it as a medicine for centuries. A causeway across Urmia's narrowest point was opened in 2008.

and depend on snowmelt and spring rains from the mountains. In summer, these riverbeds often lie dry for months. Iran's largest permanent rivers, such as the Karun, the Karkeh, and the Zayeandeh, mostly flow through the western and southern regions of the country. The wettest parts of Iran lie along the Caspian shore in the north.

Farm laborers separate grain from the chaff using traditional methods that have changed little in thousands of years. Scenes like this have become rarer as farming in Iran has become more mechanized.

(Above) Ranges of mountains and hills define much of Iran's border with its seven neighbors. Most of the larger cities lie close to these ranges. In the middle of the country lies the high and arid central plateau.

What animals are farmed in Iran?

Well suited to Iran's mountainous landscapes, sheep are by far the most important animal for Iranian farmers. Nearer to the cities, cattle play a part in Iran's large dairy industry. In rural areas, goats are an important source of protein, while donkeys, buffaloes, and even camels are bred to be worked as beasts of burden.

This pie chart shows that very little of Iran's territory is suitable for growing crops. Three-quarters of Iran is either unsuitable for farming or, at best, provides rough grazing for goats and sheep.

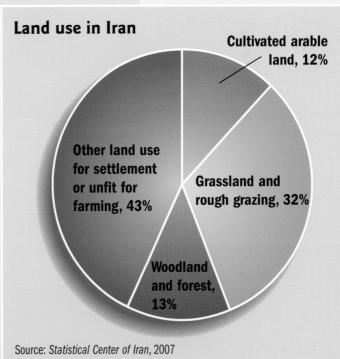

Land use in Iran

- Cultivated arable land, 12%
- Grassland and rough grazing, 32%
- Woodland and forest, 13%
- Other land use for settlement or unfit for farming, 43%

Source: *Statistical Center of Iran*, 2007

9

Many peoples

Many different peoples live in Iran, and many different languages are spoken there. About half of the population speak Persian, known as Farsi in Iran. Farsi is the official language spoken in the capital city of Tehran. However, in northwestern Iran, most people speak a very different language called Azeri, which is closer to Turkish than Farsi. A number of other languages are also spoken in Iran, including ancient tongues such as Gilaki, Mazandarani, Luri, and Balochi as well as modern Arabic and Kurdish.

A growing population

In recent decades, Iran has experienced very fast population growth. About 71 million people live in Iran today—more than double the number of 1978. Owing to a long population boom since 1980, the Iranian population is young by Western standards, with almost two-thirds of Iranians age 30 or less. Although the rate of growth in Iran's population is now slowing, the population is still expected to rise to between 90 and 100 million by 2050.

Employment in Iran

Services, 45%
Agriculture, 30%
Industry, 25%

Source: *Statistical Center of Iran*, 2007

FOCUS: CHANGING WAYS OF WORK

Since 1980, increasing numbers of Iranians have moved from the countryside to live in the rapidly growing cities. About a third of Iranians still work in agriculture, but most now earn their living in the manufacturing and service industries. About two-thirds of Iranians now live in urban areas—more than 12 million of them in Tehran alone.

Many faiths

Almost all Iranians are Muslim. Most belong to the Shia branch of Islam, which is the state religion, while fewer than 10 percent follow the Sunni Islamic tradition. There are also small communities of other believers. Christianity, Judaism, and Zoroastrianism are recognized as official religions and are tolerated to some extent. About 25,000 Iranian Jews live in Iran, mostly in Tehran, where there are 11 synagogues. A similar number keep the ancient Persian religion of Zoroastrianism alive. There are about 300,000 Christians in Iran, mostly belonging to the historic Armenian Church. There are also over 150,000 members of the Baha'i faith, but although this religion was founded in Persia, it is not recognized by the Iranian state.

Refugees and emigrants

In recent decades, large numbers of refugees have fled to Iran from troubled neighboring states. Because of wars in their own country, there are over a million Afghan refugees in Iran, mostly living in the poorest neighborhoods in the cities. There are smaller groups of refugees from Iraq, as well as Tajiks, Somalis, Bangladeshis, and Pakistanis. Political and religious changes inside Iran have also encouraged many Iranians to move overseas. There are about 2 million Iranians living in the United States and Western Europe.

Amost 70 percent of Iranians work in industry or the service sector, a statistic that reflects the move by many people from rural to urban areas.

The Zoroastrian fire temple of Pir-e Sabz at Chak Chak in central Iran lies within a mountain grotto shrine. Believers also visit the ever-dripping spring well inside the mountain. Each summer, several thousand Parsees, or Zoroastrian believers, mostly from India, make a pilgrimage here.

CHAPTER 2

History

Iran, once known as Persia, was one of the most important lands in the ancient world and the center of a great civilization. The advanced Bronze Age Elam culture developed in western Iran in about 3200 BCE. By 1000 BCE, nomadic Iranian peoples equipped with iron weapons and tools were settling in central Iran. The most powerful of these tribes was the Medes, who founded the first Iranian state in about 605 BCE.

Cyrus the Great

Cyrus, or Kuros, was a great general and lawgiver who united the Medes with the southern Persians in 549 BCE. Cyrus created a vast empire that stretched across the Middle East from the Mediterranean Sea to northern India, becoming the first shah, or "king of kings," in Persian history. For over 200 years, Cyrus and his successors ruled an empire that was feared because of its huge army and admired for its wealth and culture. Under these Achaemenid kings, Zoroastrianism became the official religion of Persia.

Greeks and Parthians

In three brief years, this first Persian empire fell to the whirlwind campaigns of Alexander the Great of Macedon (a region in northern Greece). For the next 100 years, a foreign dynasty known as the Seleucids ruled Persia, adding Greek ideas to the mix of cultures there. Over time, the lands

KEY DATES

605 BCE	The Medes establish the first Iranian empire.
559–529 BCE	Cyrus establishes the Achaemenid empire.
485 BCE	The Achaemenid empire reaches its greatest extent under Darius I and Xerxes I.
330 BCE	Alexander the Great conquers Iran.
250–224 CE	The Parthian empire flourishes.
224–651 CE	The Sassanid empire flourishes.

under Seleucid control shrank. By 200 BCE, real power in Iran lay with the Parthians, a people from the southeastern shores of the Caspian. Successful in war, the Parthian kings ruled much of southwestern Asia for 470 years. Their power only ended after defeat in a series of long and expensive wars against Rome.

The Sassanids

The Sassanids ruled Iran from 226 to 651 CE. Early Sassanid rulers such as Ardashir and Shapur I aimed to restore the Persian empire to the power it had enjoyed under Cyrus the Great. Like the Parthians, they were well-organized warriors who led large armies of heavily armored horsemen. Great Sassanid kings such as Shapur II and Khosrau I inflicted humiliating defeats on the Romans. By 620 CE, Sassanid Persia had extended its rule deep into Central Asia, to Egypt and Arabia in the west, and to northern India in the east.

Why was ancient Iran so powerful?

Iran was the home of several strong empires in ancient times. The mountainous regions produced hardy warriors, while the southern cities had the wealth and skills to make the weapons and armor needed by Persia's armies. From Cyrus on, kings could send and receive messages quickly from all parts of the empire, carried by messengers on safe roads. The Persian heartland was also a safe distance from its Greek, Roman, and Indian enemies.

Persepolis was the ancient ceremonial capital of Persia, where the emperor Darius the Great received homage from his subjects in the Apadana Palace.

The fall of the Sassanids

For over 400 years, Sassanid Persia fought against the Roman and Byzantine empires for control of the Middle East. By 620 CE, the Sassanid shahs had successfully conquered many territories that had once been part of the Roman Empire, such as Turkey, Syria, Palestine, and Egypt. The Sassanids overreached themselves, however, and the

The courtyard and reflecting pool at the Imam Mosque in Esfahan. Under the Safavid shahs, from 1500 to 1700, the capital city of Esfahan became wealthy. It was richly decorated with fabulous mosques, fine buildings, gardens, and squares.

Byzantines destroyed their army at Nineveh in 627. While still reeling from this defeat, the Sassanids were suddenly faced with another powerful enemy. Inspired by their new faith of Islam, Arab armies swept in from the south and pushed the Sassanids out of fertile Mesopotamia in the 630s. In the 650s, Arab armies passed through the Zagros Mountains and invaded the central Iranian plateau. The last Sassanid shah was killed in 651. However, rather than submit to the Arab conquerors, many Persians moved into Central Asia, helping to spread Iranian culture in that region.

A new Islamic Iran

For the next two centuries, Iran was part of a larger Arab empire, ruled by the caliph in distant Damascus or Baghdad. Nevertheless, the Iranians kept a sense of themselves as a separate people. Their language remained Farsi, not Arabic. Zoroastrianism only faded away slowly, and it was many decades before most Iranians were Muslim. Persians played a large part in running the army and the government of the caliphate. Eventually, local Persian governors began to win back power from the caliphs, and by 820, there were independent rulers again in Iran.

The golden age of Persia

The period from 850 to 1200 was a "golden age" in which the merchant cities of Iran, such as Shiraz and Esfahan, grew rich on trade and became centers of learning and the arts. At this time, Iran was part of an advanced Muslim civilization in which schools and colleges flourished. Iranian scholars such as Ibn Sina studied the sciences and made important discoveries in medicine and technology. Persian traditions in the arts, architecture, and literature were very influential and were copied throughout the Islamic world.

Mongolian invasions

This golden age ended suddenly in 1218 when the Mongolian hordes of Genghis Khan invaded Iran. More than half of the population of Iran was killed, enslaved, or died in the famines that resulted from the damage to trade and farming. The entire population of the city of Nishapur was slaughtered and their skulls piled up in great pyramids. A second Mongol invasion in the 1380s by the fierce Timurlane further weakened the once-thriving cities of Iran. Many Persian settlements only recovered their pre-invasion level of population in the later 19th century.

KEY DATES

632	The Sassanid army is defeated by Arabs at the Battle of al-Qadisiyah in Iraq.
651	The last Sassanid king is killed.
1100	Most Iranians have converted to Islam by this date.
1218	The first Mongolian invasion of Iran.
1501	Iran begins to recover under the Safavid and Qajar shahs.

Modernizing shahs

Iran's recovery began under the Safavid shahs, who ruled from 1501 to 1735. Able rulers such as Shah Abbas revived Iran's economy and modernized its army and navy. The arts flourished again in the Safavids' beautiful capital city of Esfahan. By 1700, however, Iran was increasingly affected by a shift from overland to sea trade. The precious Eastern goods, such as silks and spices, that used to pass through the markets of Iranian cities were now carried to Europe by Dutch and English trading ships. Later rulers, such as the Qajar shahs, tried to strengthen Iran by shifting the capital to Tehran and by promoting education and trade.

The Great Game

After 1800, Iran was drawn into a conflict between two foreign empires, Tsarist Russia and the British empire. Both empires used Iran in a struggle to control southwestern Asia, a struggle known in Britain as the "Great Game." In two short wars against Iran, in 1813 and 1826, Russia took control of several Iranian territories in the Caucasus region between the Black and Caspian seas. British officials at the shah's court also used their influence to get special treatment for British companies trading in Iran.

Oil!

The discovery of vast oil fields in southwestern Iran in 1908 offered the promise of great wealth. At first, however, it only made foreign powers even more determined to control Iran. The Anglo-Iranian Oil Company was given the right to exploit Iran's oil for 60 years. During World War I (1914–18), Russian and British troops occupied Iran to secure the oil supply.

Reza Shah

After World War I, Britain feared that Russia—which had transformed itself into the communist Soviet Union—would spread its ideas to Iran. The British supported an energetic soldier called Reza Khan, who marched on Tehran in 1921 with his troops and forced the government to resign. Using his power in the army, Reza put down revolts by his enemies. In 1925, he took full control of Iran and adopted the imperial title of shah.

KEY DATES

1908	Oil is discovered in Khuzestan.
1925	The Pahlavi dynasty is established.
1941–1945	The Allied occupation of Iran during World War II.
1979	The Islamic Republic of Iran is established.
1980–1988	The Iran-Iraq War.

The Pahlavi dictatorship

Reza Shah took the surname Pahlavi. He ruled as a dictator. The parliament accepted his decrees as law, and opposition newspapers were put out of business. Reza also took much of Iran's national wealth for his own personal use. However, he tried to modernize Iran by building new industries, and he attempted to lessen the influence of foreign powers over his country. He forced the Anglo-Iranian Oil Company to

Shah Mohammad Reza Pahlavi, seen here in 1953, was placed on the Iranian throne during World War II because he was willing to cooperate with the Allies against Nazi Germany. During his 38-year reign, the Western powers had great influence in Iran.

pay a larger share of its profits in taxes. He also encouraged Iranian women to wear Western-style clothes. In 1935, Reza Shah decreed that the name Iran should be used for the country instead of Persia.

Mohammad Reza Shah

In 1941, during World War II (1939–45), Britain and the Soviet Union occupied Iran to ensure that its oil did not end up in Nazi German hands. Reza Shah was forced to abdicate and was replaced by his son Mohammad Reza Pahlavi. The new shah was more pro-Western than his father, and during his reign, the United States gained great influence in Iran. In his later years, Shah Mohammad Reza Pahlavi ruled as an autocrat. Opponents were imprisoned and tortured by SAVAK, the shah's secret agents. Although his smiling image was everywhere, Iranians of all classes were hostile to his rule. After months of strikes and demonstrations, the shah went into exile in January 1979.

Islamic Republic

In February 1979, the Ayatollah Khomeini, an Islamic cleric and leading critic of the shah, returned to Tehran from exile in Paris. He was met by vast crowds of supporters. In April 1979, the country was renamed the Islamic Republic of Iran. The following year, Iran was suddenly attacked by its neighbor Iraq and found itself fighting a bitter war that lasted eight years and

The Ayatollah Ruholla Khomeini is greeted by his supporters in Tehran in February 1979. Khomeini opposed the Westernizing policies of the shah from 1963 on, suffering imprisonment and exile for his beliefs. During his long exile, he became the symbol of opposition to the shah's regime.

cost the lives of over half a million Iranians. Since 1980, Iran has been hostile to Western, and especially American, influence in the Middle East. Within Iran, the conservative Islamic clergy have great power over everyday life.

CHAPTER 3

Social Changes

Throughout Iran's long history, families in the countryside lived in a traditional way. The father was the head of the household and had great power over the other family members. Family members of different generations often lived together in one extended family unit. Older family members were respected for their wisdom and expected obedience from the young.

Today, many Iranian families, especially strictly religious ones, still hold these traditional views. In the Islamic Republic, male heads of the family have greater legal status than their wives. If a couple divorce, the father is always given custody of the children. Muslim Iranian men may take up to four wives, although most have only one wife. Among poorer and more traditional families, men still make all the important decisions while women are expected to be childbearers and homemakers.

Changing family life

Not all Iranian families live in this way. In recent decades, many better-educated women in wealthier families have gained a status more equal to their husbands'. Often this has come about because they have well-paid jobs outside the home. Educated Iranians are also having smaller families. Smaller houses and apartments in cities make it more difficult for the extended family to live together, although different generations often try to stay close to each other by living in the same neighborhood.

Since 2000, the government has tried to encourage more young Iranians to marry by staging mass weddings involving thousands of participants. Each couple taking part is given a gold coin and a copy of the Koran.

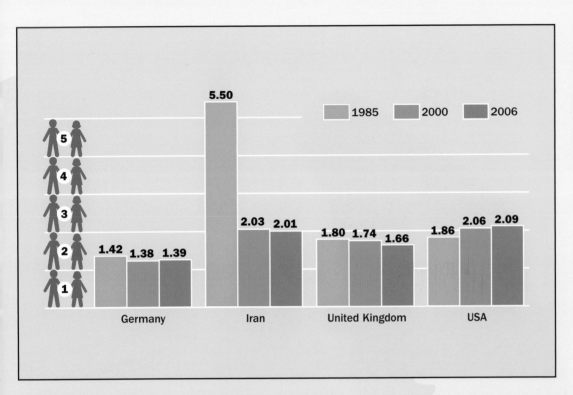

1985 2000 2006

5.50

1.42 1.38 1.39 — Germany

2.03 2.01 — Iran

1.80 1.74 1.66 — United Kingdom

1.86 2.06 2.09 — USA

In the years that followed the 1979 Islamic Revolution, Iran experienced a population boom. Fertility rates in Iran have fallen in recent years and are now more in line with those of many Western countries.

Changing ways of marriage

Marriage is important in Iran, and most young people expect to marry. Traditionally, parents have had a major say in choosing marriage partners for their children, and this is still common in many parts of Iran. However, in recent decades, some young people from educated families in the cities have had greater freedom to choose their partners.

Weddings are very expensive in Iran. The rising cost of living in recent years has also made it expensive to support a household. As a result, many young people have delayed getting married. The Islamic clergy and the government have tried to encourage marriages at an earlier age by sponsoring simple, cheap mass wedding ceremonies for thousands of young couples.

Iranian families today

Families matter a lot to most Iranians, and many people spend much of their spare time socializing with relatives. Young people often have cousins or young uncles and aunts among their close friends. The great family holiday of No Ruz, or New Year, in March is one of the high points in the Iranian year.

Family problems are seldom discussed with strangers, and at times of difficulty, Iranians look to their relatives, not the government, for help. Family connections are important and often provide a way of getting a job or a promotion. Since the Islamic Revolution, public life outside the home has become more complicated, and for many Iranians, the family has become more important as a source of security and support.

COMPARING COUNTRIES: DIVORCE

Divorce rate per 1,000 marriages, 2005–2006:

Iran	1.3
United States	4.1
United Kingdom	2.7
Germany	2.3

Sources: US Census Bureau 2005; UK Office for National Statistics, 2006; Federal Republic Statistical Office, 2006; Statistical Center of Iran, 2005.

Schools

Most Iranians highly value education. School is compulsory for all children of both sexes from the age of six to 14. Almost all schools in Iran are run by the state, and school from the elementary grades through high school is free. After five years in elementary school, children go to a middle school for two years. Here they take tests to decide if they will go on to an academic or a technical high school. Academic schools teach

Schools in Iran are more traditional than most Western schools. The pupils are strictly disciplined, sit in desks arranged in rows, and do much of their work on their own. These girls are attending a school in Tehran. In country areas, many girls do not go to school.

subjects such as literature, culture, social sciences, math, and science. Children from these schools usually go on to college. Technical schools prepare their pupils for employment in industry, business, and farming.

SCHOOL ENROLLMENT

The percentage of all Iranian children ages 14 to 17 in middle and high schools:

	Male	Female	Total
1970	42	22	32
2006	81	75	78

Source: Statistical Center of Iran

The fight for literacy

In 1950, less than a third of Iranians could read and write. Most Iranians who lived in the countryside, and most women, were illiterate. The shah's government and the Islamic Republic after 1979 both wanted to improve the industrial and technical skills of the Iranian people and knew that spreading literacy was vital. Thousands of young college students were conscripted into literacy "movements" and sent throughout Iran to teach the skills of reading and writing to people in underdeveloped areas. Others worked with adults who had missed out on school because of the upheaval during the Islamic Revolution and the war with Iraq in the 1980s. Thanks to these efforts and to high rates of enrollment in Iran's middle and high schools, only a small minority of Iranians are illiterate today.

LITERACY RATE

The percentage of all literate Iranians over 15 years of age:

	Male	Female	Total
1950 (estimated)	38	20	29
2007	88	80	84

Source: UNESCO Global Education database

Education and religion

In addition to going to the state school, many Iranian children go to weekly classes in religious instruction. Here they are taught the words of the Koran (the holy book of Islam) by experts in Muslim scripture called mullahs. Boys with a special interest in religion can progress to study Islam at special colleges of religion in the holy cities of Mashad and Qom. In the years since the 1979 revolution, state education has been increasingly influenced by religion. Since 2005, the government has put more pressure on schools to ensure that strict, conservative Islamic values are taught to children. Teachers in elementary and middle and high schools have had to give much greater time and emphasis to religious ideas and issues approved by the Islamic clergy.

Differences in learning

Schools in Iran vary greatly in quality. There is a shortage of qualified teachers in rural areas further away from the large cities. Although it is illegal for children under 15 to work, the law allows younger children in farming areas to work alongside their family. As a result, many children in the countryside do not progress beyond primary school.

Although the government provides a basic education for all young Iranians, parents in the cities often join to provide money for their local school to buy extra resources.

More than half of the population of Iran is under 25 years of age. This has caused great demand for places at good schools and the better colleges. Despite this, over 1 million students now study at Iran's universities. A 2006 survey showed that women make up 60 percent of Iran's university students.

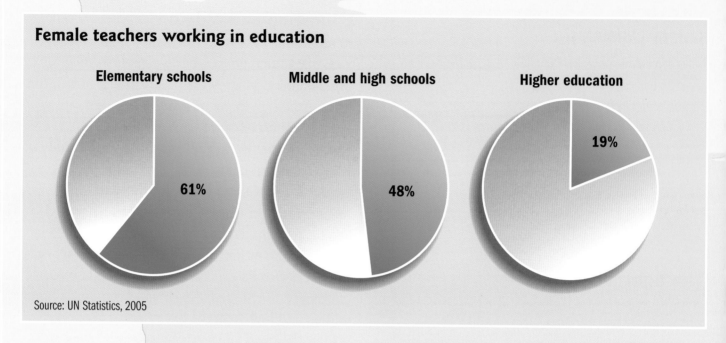

Female teachers working in education

Elementary schools — 61%

Middle and high schools — 48%

Higher education — 19%

Source: UN Statistics, 2005

Women's rights under the shah

The lives of Iranian women changed greatly under the Pahlavi shahs. Muslim women were discouraged from wearing the chador, or traditional black cloak. In the cities, younger women wore Western clothes. In 1963, Iranian women gained the right to vote, and by 1975, several women held posts in the Iranian government. However, Iranian women who opposed the shah were badly treated by his secret police.

Women under the Islamic Republic

Women played a big part in the protests that led to the overthrow of the shah in 1979. However, women have become second-class citizens in modern Iran. They do not share equal rights with men in areas such as marriage and divorce. In the courts, evidence given by a female witness only counts for half of that given by a man. Crimes against women are punished less severely than crimes against men. Women can still vote and sit in the Iranian parliament, but they can no longer do public jobs that involve making decisions, such as being a judge. In some parts of Iran, women must sit in different parts of buses from men.

Women teachers are now very common in Iranian schools. Some poorer female students work as teachers in public schools for several years after graduating. In exchange, the government pays their tuition fees.

Under wraps

Strict Muslims believe that women should cover their heads and not dress in a way that attracts attention. Since the Islamic Republic was established in 1979, women have been under pressure to cover themselves in public, using the style of clothing that is known as hijab. At first, many younger women in Iran's cities wore "light hijab." They covered their hair using small head scarves but still wore Western clothes in public.

COMPARING COUNTRIES: FEMALE LIFE EXPECTANCY

Female life expectancy at birth in years:

Germany	81.8
UK	81.1
United States	80.4
Iran	70.6

Source: World Health Organization, 2005

In recent years, however, the police have arrested women for wearing "bad hijab" in the streets. Even the few Christian and Jewish women in Iran now take care to cover themselves in the ways required by Islamic tradition.

Educated women

Since 1950, the governments of both the shah and the Islamic Republic have made great efforts to educate the women of Iran. Almost two-thirds of the students entering Iran's universities in 2007 were female. Most Iranian graduates in technical subjects such as engineering and the sciences are now female. Women increasingly hold important jobs in industry and earn higher wages than most Iranian men. Many of these educated women are unwilling to adopt the traditional roles of wife and mother expected of them in an Islamic society. After finishing their university studies, some young women in the cities are refusing to return to their parents' home. They often try to delay marriage to poorly educated men selected by their families.

Women in sports

Sports give many Iranian women an opportunity to have a life outside the home. Female race car driver Laleh Seddigh is a celebrity in Iran. However, Olympic athlete Nassim Hassanpour had to give up gymnastics because of Iran's strict dress code. Many women are choosing sports in which hijab doesn't get in the way, such as golf and shooting.

Talieh Khalkhali, the best-known female golfer in Iran, takes part in a competition in Pakistan in 2007, competing against women from other Asian nations. She wears a modest hood to hide her hair when playing but with an American-style golfing cap on top.

CHAPTER 4

Political Changes

Since the revolution in 1979, Iran has been an Islamic theocracy. This means that the country is ruled according to Islamic values and traditions. The mullahs, or Islamic clerics, have a great deal of influence over everyday life in Iran as well as over the way that the country is governed. Six Islamic clerics and six Islamic lawyers make up the powerful Council of Guardians. They decide who can sit in the Assembly of Experts, which chooses the supreme leader.

The supreme leader

The most important person in Iran is the supreme leader of the revolution. He is a highly respected religious teacher, or grand ayatollah, chosen by the leading Iranian clerics who sit in the Assembly of Experts. The supreme leader controls the armed forces of Iran and also the Islamic Revolutionary Guards, who are in charge of security inside the country. He also controls the judges and the state broadcasting of radio and television. Only the supreme leader can declare war and mobilize Iran's armed forces. Since 1979, there have been two supreme leaders of Iran.

The elected government

Iran also has an elected parliament, the Majlis, and an elected president. The president and his ministers are responsible for the day-to-day running of Iran's society and economy. The Majlis passes laws and approves the national budget. The president and members of the Majlis are elected for four-year terms by all Iranians over 15 years old. However, candidates standing for election have to be approved by the mullahs in the Council of Guardians. The guardians can also reject any laws passed by the Majlis. There are 290 seats in the Majlis, with five set aside for the minority Christian, Jewish, and Zoroastrian communities within Iran.

Political parties

There are over 200 political parties and organizations in Iran. Most of these fall into one of two opposing groups known as conservatives

FOCUS: GRAND AYATOLLAH KHOMEINI

Khomeini was a religious leader who opposed the shah's attempts to Westernize Iran. As a result, he was exiled in 1964, spending the next 15 years in Turkey, Iraq, and France. In 1978, Khomeini urged the people of Iran to strike and protest against the shah's crumbling government. Returning to Tehran once the shah had fled, Khomeini became the symbol of the Islamic Revolution. He used his influence to put down all opposition in Iran to his plans for an Islamic theocracy. He closed newspapers and outlawed political parties that defied him. He became supreme leader in 1979 and led Iran for 10 years.

President Ahmedinejad addresses the Majlis, or Iranian parliament, in August 2005, soon after his election victory.

and reformers. The conservatives believe in the Islamic constitution of Iran and get much of their support from Islamic students, the military, and the poorer people in the city and the countryside. The reformers wish to reduce the influence of the Islamic clergy and make Iran a more democratic society. However, the differences between reformers and conservatives are often slight. Both groups consist of devout Muslims who support the ideals of the Islamic Revolution. On many political issues, both groups are often in complete

agreement. Iranians who oppose the theocracy have mostly gone into exile overseas.

A number of political parties are completely forbidden within Iran. These include groups such as socialists and communists, who are especially disliked by the theocracy because they deny the existence of Allah, or God.

Khomeini's Iran

After 1979, Ayatollah Khomeini controlled Iranian society according to a strict interpretation of Islamic law and tradition. In public, Iranians—especially young people and women—had to behave in a modest way. Western influences, such as movies and pop music, were banned. Critics of the new republic were imprisoned, and many were executed. Even those who fled to the West were not safe, and several opposition leaders exiled in the United States were assassinated by supporters of the Islamic Revolution. Khomeini was especially hostile toward the United States, which he called "the Great Satan." In 1989, Khomeini declared a fatwa, or holy campaign, against writer Salman Rushdie because he believed Rushdie had been disrespectful toward Prophet Mohammed in his book *The Satanic Verses*.

However, Iran was in some ways more democratic than many states in the Middle East. All of its adult citizens, including women, were allowed to vote, and members of most other faiths were tolerated. Khomeini was genuinely popular in Iran, and many young Iranians fought willingly and with great courage in the war against Iraq from 1980 to 1988 to protect the Islamic Revolution. When Khomeini died in 1989, millions of grieving Iranians filled the streets of Tehran.

Moves for reform

In 1997, reformer Mohammed Khatami won the presidential election, gaining almost 70

The current supreme leader of Iran, Ayatollah Khamenei, casts his vote in the 2008 elections for the Majlis. Khamenei has used his influence to support conservative politicians and parties. The 2008 elections were won by conservatives after many reformist candidates were banned from standing for election.

Since the 2004 elections, conservative parties and factions have enjoyed a clear majority in the Majlis, although not all conservative members of the parliament support President Ahmadinejad.

percent of the vote. Khatami was a mullah, but he had lived in Germany and spoke several Western languages. He introduced a mild program of reform, permitting slightly more freedom of speech and reducing the interference of the mullahs and their supporters in the daily life of Iranians. He was supported by many young voters and by those women who resented the way their lives had changed under the Islamic Republic. Khatami won a second term as president in 2001, securing an even larger share of the vote. After 2000, many reformers were also elected to the Majlis.

The failure of the reformers

Although he won two elections, President Khatami was unable to bring about much change in Iran. Islamic conservatives wanted to keep Iran the way it had been under Ayatollah Khomeini. They disliked Khatami's plans to give more freedom of expression to writers and the press. They also believed he would allow Western influences back into the country. The conservative Council of Guardians vetoed laws proposed by Khatami and the reformers in the Majlis. The new supreme leader, Ayatollah Khamenei, was against change and used his powers to ban newspapers that supported Khatami's ideas.

In the elections of 2004 and 2008, the Council of Guardians used its power to ban thousands of candidates, mostly reformers, from standing for election. As a result, conservative candidates won most of the seats in the Majlis. In 2005, Khatami came to the end of his term as president. His successor was the conservative Mahmoud Ahmadinejad.

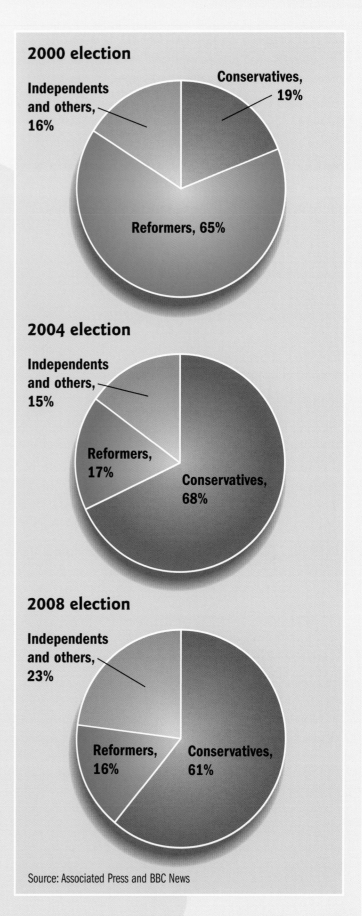

2000 election

Independents and others, 16%

Conservatives, 19%

Reformers, 65%

2004 election

Independents and others, 15%

Reformers, 17%

Conservatives, 68%

2008 election

Independents and others, 23%

Reformers, 16%

Conservatives, 61%

Source: Associated Press and BBC News

Control and opposition in Iran

Since 1979, the government of Iran has defended the values of the Islamic Revolution very forcefully. The police and state security agencies have been used to break up strikes and protests. Other groups in Iran have also been active in putting down political and social dissent. These groups include Islamic students from Koranic schools and members of the Basij, or volunteer militias. Although they are not official organizations, the militias support the government by enforcing its strict code of public behavior and by attacking individuals and groups who criticize the regime.

Repression

During Mohammad Khatami's period as president, from 1999 to 2005, the government permitted some public demonstrations. In recent years, however, strikers and protestors have been beaten and arrested by the police and sentenced to long terms in prison. Since 2006, students with liberal views have been barred from entering higher education, while university teachers suspected of disloyalty to the regime have been suspended and fired from their jobs. Campaigners for social reform, such as women's rights activists, have also been persecuted.

Human rights

Iran has been seriously criticized by international organizations, including the United Nations, for its restrictions on freedom of speech and abuses of human rights. They have criticized the harsh punishments that are used in Iran, such as hanging, flogging, and the amputation of limbs. These punishments are not just used against criminals but against people who are accused of offending the moral code of Islam, such as adulterers, homosexuals, and those who abandon their Islamic faith. In 2008, an Iranian refugee

FOCUS: CENSORSHIP

Since 2000, dozens of newspapers that were critical of the government have been closed down and members of the Basij have attacked journalists and ransacked their homes. The government also blocks access to websites that it considers undesirable and "un-Islamic." Bloggers, or online journalists, have been imprisoned. Experts believe the regime is now building a "national internet" in order to control all online activity by Iranians. It hopes to keep out all Western ideas and values as well as propaganda from exiled Iranians who oppose the Islamic regime in Tehran.

who was refused permission to stay in the United Kingdom desperately pleaded not to be sent back to Iran. If he was deported there, he believed that he would be publicly executed for being gay.

Iranian exiles

There are over 4 million Iranians living outside Iran, mostly in Turkey, the Gulf states, Europe, and North America. Many of these exiles belong to groups that oppose the Iranian government and who have different hopes for the future of their country. Some want to bring about a more democratic Iran, while others belong to outlawed socialist and communist parties. There are also monarchist groups that want to restore the Pahlavi shahs. These exile groups have had little impact, however, not least because there is still a great deal of genuine popular support for the Islamic Revolution inside Iran.

The largest community of Iranian exiles is in the United States. Most of the Iranians who fled there after 1979 were wealthy, educated people who had skills in science and business. Under the shahs, they had adopted Western ways of living and held moderate views on religion and politics.

Others were from minority groups, such as Kurds and Armenians, who feared persecution in the Islamic Republic. Many of these exiles have been very successful in their adopted countries.

Public politics

Politics in Iran are often played out in the streets of Tehran and the other large cities. The government frequently organizes large demonstrations to show the extent of public support for its policies. Students and members of the militias play a large part in these demonstrations. Compared to most Western countries, it is also much more common for leading Iranian politicians to address large crowds of their supporters in the open air. Large posters and banners are also used to spread the government's message.

Propaganda images in the streets of Iran often demonize Western powers, especially the United States. This wall painting of the Statue of Liberty as a deathly skull was daubed on the wall of the former US Embassy in Tehran. Demonstrations against Western powers are still regularly held here.

CHAPTER 5

Economic Changes

Much of the Iranian economy is controlled by the state. Under the Pahlavi shahs and in the early years of the Islamic Republic, the government put a great deal of effort into large-scale projects such as building dams, roads, and pipelines. These were designed to improve the nation's infrastructure. Today, the state owns companies in all the key industries, such as oil and gas, metals, and car manufacturing. Communication industries, such as telephone services, aviation, and railroads, are also under state control. Experts estimate that more than two-thirds of the Iranian economy is in the state sector.

Privatization

Following the Islamic Revolution, many skilled managers and engineers fled Iran, weakening the economy. Further economic damage was inflicted during the war with Iraq in the 1980s, when major centers of industrial production in western Iran were bombed. After the war, reformers in the Majlis wanted to privatize some state-owned companies, believing this would help Iran's ailing economy. However, conservatives in the government opposed this move, not wishing to lose control over the Iranian economy. Members of the Islamic Revolutionary Guard, who had taken important positions in state-owned companies, were also against these changes.

Rising oil values

Oil and gas production is the most important industry in Iran. Iran is the fourth-largest producer of oil in the world and has the second-largest reserves of natural gas. Petroleum alone accounts for almost 80 percent

Former Iranian president Mohammad Khatami surveys the offshore oil rig at Forouzan. Since 2000, much of Iran's oil has come from offshore drilling platforms that exploit the reserves of oil under the waters of the Persian Gulf.

Iran is a major producer of crude oil, but much of its oil has to be sold to other countries that are better able to turn the oil into other products such as gasoline.

Average daily production of crude oil in 2006

Sources: OPEC and US Economic Information Administration

of the value of Iran's exports. In the 1980s, Iran tried to reduce the scale of its oil and gas production to conserve its stocks for the long term. However, production soon increased again when Iranian oil companies discovered new fields in the waters of the Persian Gulf off the Iranian coast. Since 2000, Iran has earned vast amounts of foreign currency—possibly more than $70 billion—thanks to the rising price of oil and gas products on world markets.

Inefficiency

Since 1979, the Iranian government has been highly dependent on oil exports. Iran produces over 4 million barrels of oil every day, and nearly 40 percent of that oil is used to fuel the domestic economy. Almost half of the national budget comes from oil and gas revenues. However, industry experts believe that the Iranian oil industry is very inefficient. It is easy to extract oil in the flatlands of Khuzestan, but elsewhere the infrastructure for transporting oil and gas is poor. Not enough money has been invested in exploring for new fields. Because oil is plentiful within Iran, however, it is often used in an inefficient way. Iran has been slow to adopt new, more efficient technologies, both in extracting and using its fossil fuels.

PROVEN RESERVES OF NATURAL GAS (2003–2004)

	Reserves in billion cubic feet	Rank in the world
Russia	1,655,810	1st
Iran	937,118	2nd
Quatar	880,750	3rd
United Arab Emirates	211,380	4th
United States	192,035	5th
UK	20,785	32nd
Germany	9,864	42nd

Source: *Oil and Gas Journal*, 2006

New energies

Over 93 percent of Iran's electricity comes from burning oil and gas. Hydroelectric schemes provide the remainder. However, Iran has begun to develop alternative sources of energy. Stations that harness geothermal energy and wind power have opened in recent years. A solar power plant is due to open in 2009, and a nuclear plant will open at Bushehr on the southwest coast in 2008.

Budget problems

Since the revolution, the rise in population has led to ever-increasing numbers of young Iranians looking for jobs. However, industry in Iran has not been able to grow fast enough to provide sufficient employment. This is partly due to government resistance to new Western ideas and technologies. Iranian governments have also struggled to balance their budgets. Although oil exports bring in vast revenues, the government spends heavily on subsidies to keep down the rising cost of everyday needs such as gas and electricity. The government also subsidizes wheat and other key foodstuffs, as well as materials such as steel and cement, needed for the building industry. Another problem has been the continuing fall in the value of Iran's currency. In 1978, 70 Iranian rials bought one dollar. In 2008, a dollar was worth over 9,000 rials.

Iranian public spending in 2006 as a percentage of total government expenditure

Health care, 6%

Education, 16%

Subsidies on essential products, e.g., gasoline, 37%

Social provision, including pensions, 23%

Defense and public order, 9%

Interest on public debt, 2%

Capital infrastructure projects, 7%

Source: Statistical Center of the Islamic Republic of Iran

Diversification

Someday in the future, Iran's oil will run out. The government is therefore trying to use some of its income from oil and gas to develop a range of different industries. This is called diversification. Iran is encouraging new technological industries that make use of its well-educated and highly skilled workforce rather than traditional industries that make products that are often difficult to sell in foreign markets. One example is the Iranian arms industry, which sold sophisticated weapons worth over $100 million to over 50 countries in 2006. Other emerging industries in Iran include consumer electronics, aerospace and communications, pharmaceuticals, industrial robotics, and nuclear technology.

The Five Year Plan, 2005–10

The government of President Ahmadinejad is conservative in religious and cultural affairs. However, it is trying to change and modernize Iran's economy. In its Five Year Plan, launched in 2005, it hopes to sell more Iranian products overseas and build on Iran's existing markets in Asian countries such as Japan, China, and South Korea. Ahmadinejad's government has also borrowed Western economic ideas, such as setting up science and technology parks to attract foreign investors. Another aim of the plan is to develop a "national internet" in Iran that will make it easier for the authorities to police what people look at on the Internet. Only sites that are acceptable to the authorities will be available to Iranian computer users.

Self-sufficiency

The government also hopes to make Iran as self-sufficient as possible and limit the import of

The Iranian government spends more than a third of its annual budget in subsidies to keep down the cost of everyday necessities such as food and fuel.

expensive goods from abroad. Iranian automakers already sell over 90 percent of the vehicles driven there. Almost all the medicines used in Iran are produced locally. Iran also has thousands of small factories and workshops, often run as family businesses. Here, craftspeople make textiles, carpets, glassware, ceramics, and many other products. Since these skills are passed on through families, the products made by these local craftspeople are often of a very high quality. After many large factories in western Iran were damaged in the war with Iraq, there was a surge in demand for products made in small workshops and sold in local markets.

Food and raw materials

In recent years, Iran has begun to reach its goal of self-sufficiency in foodstuffs. In 2007, for the first

Although Iran has many large, modern factories, craftspeople in small workshops, such as this potter, continue to play an important part in the Iranian economy. These crafts often add to the income of farming families in rural areas.

time, it produced more wheat than it needed and was able to sell the surplus overseas. Iran now exports a wide range of natural and processed foods to Turkey, Central Asia, and the Middle East, which brings in over $1 billion each year. Iran also has rich deposits of valuable minerals such as coal, gold, copper, and uranium. It lacks the money and the technology to exploit these resources but is looking to attract investors from trading partners such as Germany and China, who have experience in these industries.

CHAPTER 6

Environmental Changes

Tehran is one of the most polluted cities in the world. The city is often covered in thick clouds of smog, a mixture of pollutants and fog, which make the air difficult to breathe. On windless days, the pollution often remains hovering in the clouds above the city. Tehran's smog has many causes, from domestic fires in winter to the fumes released by factories and workshops throughout the year. Above all, the streets of Tehran are heavily congested with cars.

Many citizens of Tehran and other Iranian cities regularly wear "smog masks"—gauze face masks—in public so that they do not breathe in dangerous toxins and other pollutants.

ANNUAL IRANIAN CARBON EMISSIONS

1980	36.4 million tons
2000	88.9 million tons

Source: *US Dept of Energy International Pollution Report*, 2002

Many commuters have little choice but to drive since the city has poor systems of public transportation. As a result of this congestion and pollution, the level of toxins in the Tehran air has been recorded at three times the acceptable level for human health.

Gas heads

One of the problems is that gas in Iran is very cheap at about 39 cents per gallon (10 cents per liter)—about a fifth of its real cost—thanks to generous government subsidies. This has encouraged Iranians to drive more and consume more gas than car owners in most other countries. Iranian cars are also often made from older, less fuel-efficient designs. Until 2003, most still used leaded gas and often lacked equipment to control their emissions.

Cleaning up Tehran

In June 2007, the government announced that drivers would be allowed to buy a maximum of 26 gallons (100 liters) of gas each month. Taxi drivers were given a 206-gallon (800-liter) allowance because, by carrying passengers, they could help reduce overall fuel consumption. Many Tehran inhabitants were angered by this plan because they believed they were entitled to cheap, unlimited gas. Without sufficient petrol in a city with poor public transportation, they were unable to move around and get to work. Some Tehran drivers even rioted when they heard the news, angry that they were given just two hours' notice of the restrictions. Twelve gas stations were burned down.

Public transportation

In 2005, the government began to tackle the problem of poor air quality in Iran's cities. New laws are forcing automakers to install modern catalytic converters in their models. Older laws restricting cars from entering city centers are being enforced more rigorosly. Taxis and buses are being converted to run on cleaner fuels, such as natural gas. Tehran's underground railway, opened in 2001, is being extended, and similar mass transit rail systems are planned for other Iranian cities. In early 2008, a slight improvement was recorded in Tehran's air quality.

International cooperation

Iran shares some of its environmental problems with its neighbors. Iran has agreed to support United Nations goals for improving the environment but has been slow to actually make improvements within Iran or to work with other countries on schemes for environmental improvement. This is due in part to Iran's political isolation. To solve complex international environmental problems, such as the high levels of air and water pollution caused by the oil industry, Iran will have to learn to cooperate more with its neighbors.

FOCUS: THE HUMAN COST OF AIR POLLUTION

Because of the poor air quality in Tehran, lung disease is common in the city. In 2005, almost 10,000 Iranians died from diseases caused by air pollution. In December of that year, schools in Tehran were closed and children were kept indoors so they would not breathe in the toxic fumes. Hospitals in Tehran reported hundreds of smog victims. People in other cities in Iran also suffer regularly from poor air quality, often caused by pollution from oil refineries.

Habitat under pressure

Increasingly, human settlements are encroaching on the Iranian countryside. As cities expand, farmland is giving way to housing and industrial developments. The famous orchards of Tehran, traditionally the green lungs of the city, have mostly disappeared. In more remote areas, far

The Persian fallow deer is a native of the woodlands of Khuzestan in southern Iran. By the 1980s, it had been almost driven to extinction through hunting and habitat destruction. It remains critically endangered.

from the cities, drought, deforestation, and salination have changed the landscape, harming animal and human life.

VANISHING WETLANDS

Higher average summer temperatures and human exploitation of water resources are threatening Iran's wetlands. One example is the Hamun-e-Helmand wetlands on Iran's southeastern border with Afghanistan. Historically, this area of marshes and small lakes covered about 624 sq mi (1,600 square km) and supported a wide range of wildlife and several fishing villages. By 2001, however, the wetlands had almost completely dried up, leaving only a dry, dusty basin. The Iranian government believes that Afghan farmers across the border have diverted much of the water from the Helmand River, which used to feed into the wetlands.

Drought and desertification

Large areas of Iran's highlands have suffered prolonged periods of drought in recent years. This has led to a spread of desert conditions, or desertification. This situation has been caused, in part, by climate change, which has increased average summer temperatures. In eastern and central Iran, summer temperatures of 97 to 102°F (36 to 39°C) are now common, while rainfall in some areas has fallen to less than 7.8 inches (200 mm) per year. Fresh drinking water in many remote areas of Iran has become increasingly scarce. Human activity is also partly to blame for the spreading deserts. Farmers have overgrazed their flocks on pastures that were already dry and thin. Their animals eat the remaining vegetation and break up the dry soil with their hooves. Much of this broken, dusty topsoil then gets blown away by the wind, creating barren desert.

Water pollution

Since about 1990, settlements to house poorer people have sprung up on the edges of cities and in the countryside. These settlements have been hurriedly built and often lack proper systems for disposing of wastewater and sewage. As a result, sewage and liquid waste often run off into the groundwater, contaminating rivers and lakes. Coastal waters in the Persian Gulf and the Caspian Sea have also been contaminated by oil and chemical spills, as well as by effluent from oil refineries and factories.

Endangered wildlife

Pollution and the shrinking wilderness have seriously affected the wildlife of Iran. The Baluchistan, or black Asian, bear is now an endangered species in Iran, owing to the logging of forests, which has reduced its ability to find food. Overfishing and maritime pollution have caused several species of turtle, including the hawksbill, almost to disappear from the Persian Gulf. The long-legged Siberian white crane is gradually dying out in Iran as its wetland habitat shrinks. In all, conservationists list 20 mammal species and 14 bird species in Iran as endangered.

This former nomadic sheepherder was forced to make a permanent home here in eastern Iran, close to a source of water, after drought hit the region and killed off his sheep and goats.

CHAPTER 7

Changing Relationships

Since 1979, many countries around the world have viewed revolutionary Iran as a threat to the stability of the Middle East. On several occasions, the United Nations Security Council has passed sanctions, or limitations on trade, to try to force Iran to stop developing its weapons technology. However, Iran argues that it is acting lawfully in its own defense. It has also vigorously defended its own territorial rights, confronting British and American warships that have (according to Iran) strayed into Iranian waters.

Iran and the United States

Under the Pahlavi shahs, the United States exercised a great deal of influence in Iran. However, since the Islamic Revolution of 1979, Iran and the United States have been deeply suspicious of each other. The Iranian government believes that the United States has too much influence in the Middle East and has tried to undermine Iran. During the 1980s war between Iran and Iraq, for example, the United States supplied Iraq with military equipment and satellite intelligence.

The United States fears Iran's growing power in the region and its support for Islamist organizations such as Hezbollah in Lebanon and Hamas in Gaza. These groups have carried out terrorist attacks against Israel, a strong ally of the United States in the region. The United States is concerned that a strong Iran could alter the balance of power in the Middle East and threaten the West's oil supply. In 2002, President George W. Bush named Iran as one of three countries that, together with North Korea and Iraq, formed an "axis of evil."

Nuclear tensions

In 1975, the shah's government began building a nuclear power plant to provide electricity near Bushehr in southwest Iran. The reactor was damaged by Iraqi air attacks during the 1980s, but the Iranians began reconstructing it in 1995. The United States fears that Iran will use the reactor to make enriched uranium, the material used in

CASE STUDY: IRAN AND ISRAEL

Iran has been hostile toward Israel since the 1979 revolution and gives support to anti-Israeli militant groups such as Hezbollah and Hamas. In 2005, President Ahmadinejad declared that Israel should "be wiped off the map." Iranian government officials later said that Ahmadinejad had been mistranslated and claimed that Iran only wants to see a fair settlement for the displaced Palestinian people. However, Israel views Iran as its main enemy in the region. Military experts believe that Israel has plans to destroy Iran's nuclear installations if there is evidence that the Iranians have built nuclear weapons.

Supporters of the militant Islamist organization Hezbollah demonstrate in Lebanon in 2006. Iran supports Hezbollah in its struggle against Israel. Iran's defiantly anti-Israeli stance is popular among many ordinary Muslims but a source of tension between Iran and the West.

nuclear weapons. Iran claims that the reactor will only be used to create nuclear power to supply the country's energy needs. If Iran develops nuclear weapons, it will breach the Nuclear Nonproliferation Treaty, an international agreement designed to stop more countries from building these weapons. In March 2007, the United Nations imposed tough sanctions on Iran to discourage its nuclear program. In November,

American intelligence reports judged that Iran had halted its nuclear weapons program in 2003 and would probably not have enough material for a bomb until after 2015.

Waterway clash

The Shatt al-Arab is a river that forms part of the border between Iraq and Iran. Since the invasion of Iraq by a Western coalition in 2003, Iran has kept a close watch on American and British forces in the area. In 2007, Iranian warships surrounded the British ship *Cornwall* near the mouth of the Shatt al-Arab. Fifteen members of the Royal Navy were detained and only released after a diplomatic crisis.

Crisis in Iraq

In 2003, the United States and other Western powers invaded Iraq to overthrow the regime of dictator Saddam Hussein. The United States also wanted to secure the flow of oil from Iraq and build a strong military base in the region close to Iran's borders. At first, Iran was fearful of the US presence in the region. By 2008, however, it was increasingly clear that events in Iraq had weakened American prestige in the Middle East. Shia militias, equipped and supported by Iran, continued to undermine American efforts to bring stability to Iraq.

Neighboring Gulf states

The Arab states on the Persian Gulf—Saudi Arabia, Bahrain, Kuwait, Qatar, Oman, and the United Arab Emirates—have an uneasy relationship with Iran. As oil producers, they

Iraqi supporters of the radical Shia cleric Moqtada al-Sadr celebrate the destruction of a US army truck in Baghdad in 2004. Al-Sadr has built a formidable force, the Mahdi Army, which resists the foreign occupation from its stronghold in the Shia district of Baghdad. He has received funds and weapons from Iran.

want stable relations with Western powers and become anxious when Iranian leaders talk about using the oil supply as a "weapon against the West." Also, the governments of these Arab states are Sunni Muslims, with different religious traditions from the Shia Muslims of Iran. They fear the growing influence of Shia Iran, especially among the Shia minorities who live in their own lands, often in the richest oil-producing regions.

Jordan and Egypt

The government of Jordan is pro-Western, but most of Jordan's population is of Palestinian

EXPANDING IRANIAN EXPORTS
(IN BILLIONS OF DOLLARS)

	1996	2006
China	3.58	59.1
India	5.90	78.8
Russia	0.85	16.6

Source: Statistical Center of Iran; US Energy Information Administration; *OPEC World Oil Outlook*

Iran and Russia

Russia has strong economic interests in Iran, having invested in Iranian nuclear power development, aviation, and gas exploration. Russia and Iran are also working together to develop better road and rail links in the region to help the growth of trade between the two nations. The two powers are not in agreement on all matters, however. Russia does not support Iran's hopes of formally dividing the territory of the Caspian Sea. Iran wants a fifth share of the sea and its mineral resources, although it only occupies 12 percent of the Caspian coastline.

New friends

Since 1998, China has become a major trading partner of Iran, and over 100 Chinese companies now operate there. Some are involved in major infrastructure projects, such as building airports and roads, while others sell consumer goods. Iran has signed agreements with China worth over $100 billion to supply China with oil and gas.

Indian companies are also looking to import gas from southern Iran by pipeline.

origin. Many ordinary Jordanians view Iran, with its anti-Israel stance, as a greater champion of the Palestinian cause than their own government. The Jordanian government fears the growth of support for Iranian-backed Islamist groups among its own population and among the many Iraqi refugees who have arrived in Jordan since the 2003 invasion. In the same way, the Egyptian government has been embarrased by Iran's active support for Hezbollah and Hamas, both of which are popular in the streets and bazaars of Egypt.

President Ahmadinejad of Iran met with President Vladimir Putin of Russia in 2007 to discuss cooperation among the countries that surround the land-locked Caspian Sea. Putin has sometimes acted as a go-between when there have been diplomatic disputes between Iran and the Western powers.

CHAPTER 8

Future Challenges

One of the major challenges facing Iran today is a growing inequality within Iranian society. Since 2000, the gap between the incomes of the wealthiest and poorest sections of the population has become much wider. Unemployment in the cities has risen steeply. And while the prices of everyday goods have increased, the wages of most Iranian workers have stayed the same or been eaten away by inflation. Many ordinary Iranian families struggle to stay above the official poverty line. There are signs of tension in the streets because of these economic problems, with a growing number of strikes and protests by discontented workers. More positively, some of the Basij, or volunteer militias, are beginning to get involved in economic projects designed to help people who live in the poorest areas of Iran's cities.

Brain drain

In the years since 1979, many well-educated young Iranians left their homeland to live abroad. Many others are desperate to leave. Some have left because they resent the way that the government controls daily life in Iran and they want to lead freer lives. However, most just want better-paid jobs and careers. Many of these "economic exiles" complain that inside Iran, the best jobs are often given to those with family connections to the government rather than to the best-qualified applicants. There is already a shortage of skilled managers with the business skills needed to run Iran's industries. This "brain drain" is estimated to cost the Iranian economy over $30 billion every year.

Controlling information

Changes in technology are making it more difficult for the Iranian government to control information within the country. The government runs broadcasting within Iran, but many Iranians have satellite dishes that can pick up television stations from around the world. Some of these stations are run by opponents of the Iranian government. The government attempts to control the Internet, but most middle-class Iranians have access to the web at home and the government finds it difficult to police the many blogs that spring up. After a recent demonstration at Tehran University, the authorities claimed that only a few students had taken part in the protest, but images captured on cell phones and posted online showed that this was not true.

American encirclement

Since the Islamic Revolution, Iran has viewed the United States as its greatest enemy. Under President Bush, the United States has established a major military presence in the region by placing large numbers of troops in Iraq, Turkey, and Afghanistan. Also, the governments of Turkmenistan, Azerbaijan, and Pakistan have offered the United States the use of military bases in their countries. This American presence in six of its neighbors worries the Iranian government, and many ordinary Iranians fear a US military invasion of their country. Some also fear that President Ahmadinejad is too confrontational and that his open hostility toward Israel and the West might eventually lead to conflict.

Competing visions
Within Iran, there are differing visions of the future of the country. Iranian reformers, and their supporters, want to adopt some features of a freer, more democratic way of life. Conservative Iranians, however, are determined to remain faithful to the strict Islamic ideals of the 1979 revolution. Resolving the conflict between these two visions is probably the greatest challenge facing the Iranian people in the early twenty-first century.

Iranian schoolgirls chat online at an Internet café that is exclusively for females. Daily life in Iran is influenced by ancient Islamic traditions as well as the technology of the modern world.

Timeline

605 BCE The Medes establish the first Iranian empire.

559–529 BCE Cyrus establishes the Achaemenid empire.

485 BCE The Achaemenid Empire reaches its greatest extent under Darius I and Xerxes I.

330 BCE Alexander the Great conquers Iran.

250–224 CE The Parthian empire flourishes.

224–651 The Sassanid empire flourishes.

632 The Sassanid army is defeated by Arabs at the Battle of al-Qadisiyah in Iraq.

651 The last Sassanid king is killed.

1100 Most Iranians have converted to Islam by this date.

1218 The first Mongolian invasion of Iran.

1501 Iran begins to recover under the Safavid and Qajar shahs.

1908 Oil is discovered in Khuzestan.

1925 The Pahlavi dynasty is established.

1941–45 The Allies occupy Iran during World War II.

1953 The government of Iran is overthrown by a US plot.

1963 Iranian women get the vote.

January 1979 The shah goes into exile overseas.

February 1979 Ayatollah Khomeini returns to Iran from exile. The Islamic Republic of Iran is established.

1980 Saddam Hussein's Iraq attacks Iran.

1988 The Iran-Iraq War ends.

1989 Ayatollah Khomeini dies.

1995 The damaged nuclear power station at Bushehr is reconstructed.

1997 Reformer Mohammed Khatami is elected president of Iran.

2000 Reformers win a majority of seats in the Iranian Majlis.

2002 President George W. Bush declares Iran part of the "axis of evil."

2003 The United States and its allies invade and occupy neighboring Iraq.

2004 Most seats in the Majlis are won by conservatives.

2005 Conservative Mahmoud Ahmadinejad is elected president of Iran.

2006 The government launches a new crackdown on its opponents.

2007 The government introduces gas rationing.

2008 In elections, the conservatives keep control of the Majlis.

Glossary

abdicate Give up power.

academic Traditional school subjects, such as math, science, and literature.

activist Someone who campaigns in support of his or her political beliefs.

autocrat The sole ruler of a state, who makes all decisions alone.

ayatollah Title given to senior Shia clerics, meaning "sign of God."

caliph Title given to the Muslim rulers between 650 and 1200.

causeway A land bridge across a stretch of water.

clergy The class of priests in a country.

cleric A priest or religious official.

conscripted Forced to join something, such as an army or some other organized movement or force.

conservative Someone who prefers things to stay as they are.

constitution The body of laws that determine how a country is governed.

decree A law anounced by a dictator or autocrat.

dictator A ruthless leader who suppresses opponents.

discrimination Unfair or unequal treatment.

dissent Disagree, usually with a government.

diversification A policy followed by a government or commercial organization to expand into new industries.

effluent Pollution, usually in liquid form.

emissions Pollution, usually in the form of gases.

geothermal energy Heat obtained from beneath the earth's surface.

humid Warm, moist weather conditions.

illiterate Unable to read or write.

infrastructure The basic systems and structures that are needed to run a country.

Koran The Muslim holy book.

militia Semi-official groups of volunteers who take on policing duties.

nomadic Moving from place to place.

pastures Land on which farmers graze their livestock.

plateau High, flat land.

proliferation The spread of something.

reformer Someone who wants to improve or change things.

scripture Sacred writings.

Shia The Muslim tradition followed by most Iranians.

status The social and legal standing of an individual.

subsidies Government money used to keep down the price of goods.

Sunni The Muslim tradition followed in most Arab countries.

synagogues Jewish places of worship.

theocracy A state where the leaders are priests.

veto The power of one branch of government to reject the laws passed by another.

Further information

Books

Dicker, Katie. *Looking at Countries: Iran*. Franklin Watts, 2008.

Fast, April. *Lands, Peoples and Cultures: Iran, the Land*. Crabtree Publishers, 2005.

Lyle, Garry. *Iran*. Chelsea House Publishers, 1997.

Richter, Joanne. *Lands, Peoples and Cultures: Iran, the Culture*. Crabtree Publications, 2006.

Taus-Bolstad, Stacy. *Visual Geography: Iran in Pictures*. Lerner Publications, 2005.

Websites

www.parstimes.com
News and information about contemporary Iran.

www.persia.org
A website with links to other sites on the history and geography of Iran.

www.news.bbc.co.uk/1/hi/world/middle_east/country-profiles/790877.stm
This site provides an overview of Iran, key facts and events, leader profiles, and current news.

Index

Page numbers in **bold** refer to illustrations and charts.